Toward Coexistence:
An Analysis of the Resolutions
of the Palestine National Council

Institute for Palestine Studies
Georgetown Station
P.O. Box 25697
Washington, D.C. 20007
(202) 342-3990

The Institute for Palestine Studies (IPS) is an independent, non-profit Arab research and publication center, with offices in Washington, D.C., London, Paris, Nicosia, and Beirut.

Opinions expressed in IPS publications do not necessarily reflect those of the Institute.
Copyright © 1990 by the
Institute for Palestine Studies
ISBN 0-88728-210-5
Library of Congress Catalog Card Number:
90-081685

TOWARD COEXISTENCE

An Analysis of the Resolutions of the Palestine National Council

MUHAMMAD MUSLIH

The Institute for Palestine Studies
Washington, D.C.

CONTENTS

Executive Summary vii

Toward Coexistence: An Analysis of the Resolutions of the Palestine National Council 1
   The PNC 4
   The Total Liberation Phase: The First Four PNCs 9
   The Secular Democratic State Phase: The Fifth through Eleventh PNCs 17
   The Two-State Solution Phase (The Twelfth through Nineteenth PNCs, June 1974 to November 1988) 23

Chronology 39

Notes 54

EXECUTIVE SUMMARY

Since December, 1988, the United States has been carrying on a dialogue with the PLO as a major step toward the resolution of the Palestine problem and the Arab/Israeli conflict. This dialogue was opened shortly after Yasir Arafat's statements of December 14, 1988—in which he recognized the state of Israel, accepted UN Security Council Resolution 242 and the principle of a two-state solution, and renounced terrorism. More than 100 countries now recognize the PLO as the representative of the Palestinians and many have responded positively to its declaration in November, 1988 of a Palestinian state based on coexistence with Israel. Many Israelis, also, realize that any solution must involve the PLO. Yet, despite the PLO's statements and the international recognition that it enjoys, there are those who would exclude it from negotiations, because, they argue, the PLO is not sincere in seeking a peaceful settlement.

The best test of whether Arafat's statements truly represent a genuine movement toward peace and Palestinian/Israeli coexistence is to compare them with the other main statements of the Palestinian community: the resolutions of the Palestine National Council, the highest policy-making body of the PLO, which the Palestinians and most of the world regard as a Palestinian parliament in exile. Such a comparison would reveal the profound and consistent evolution towards pragmatism in the PLO's attitude towards

Israel. This evolution is manifest in the resolutions taken in the successive meetings of the PNC since its first meeting in 1964.

Examination of the PNC resolutions reveals three phases in the evolution of Palestinian thinking about the conflict with Israel. Each transition from one phase to the next involved a re-formulation of Palestinian objectives and an increasing reliance on diplomatic means for achieving them.

These phases are:

- the "total liberation" phase, from 1964 through 1968, during which the PLO was committed to regaining Palestinians' sovereignty over their entire original homeland and believed that armed struggle was the only way to do so. It envisioned a liberated Palestine as an Arab state in which all Jewish residents who had lived in Palestine prior to 1947 (the year in which the UN General Assembly recommended the partition of Palestine) would have citizenship;

- the "secular democratic state" phase, from 1969 through 1973. In this phase the PLO continued to stress the importance of armed struggle and reject the partition of Palestine. However, it placed new emphasis on the specifically Palestinian (rather than Arab) character of the country and held out the hope that Palestine could be shared by all citizens, whether Jewish, Christian or Muslim, on the basis of non-sectarian principles (democracy, equality and mutual respect). Although Zionist institutions would be dismantled, Jewish Palestinians would have the same rights as other citizens, regardless of the date of their arrival in Palestine. A burgeoning tendency to employ diplomatic as well as military means to achieve these goals appeared;

- the "two-state solution" phase, which began in 1974 and culminated in the acceptance of a Palestinian state alongside Israel, not as a transitional stage but as a *point final*. The strategy during much of this phase has been to concentrate on diplomatic efforts at the expense of military efforts, to contact moderate Israeli groups and individuals directly, to insist on PLO participation in a Middle East peace conference and affirm the PLO's readiness to open a direct dialogue with the Israeli government.

As this study makes clear, the stance of the early PNCs, which emphasized armed struggle and the total liberation of Palestinian land, has been gradually superseded by much more accommodating positions. Without doubt, the most important influence on the first PNC resolutions was the War of 1948 itself, during which almost two-thirds of the Palestinian people were either forcibly displaced or left in panic and became refugees, living in exile. The moral basis, then, to the absolute rejection of Israel's legitimacy in the early PNC resolutions was the perception that the premises of Zionism were based on a denial of Palestinian national rights, culminating in the injustice of 1948. The repetition of this tragedy in 1967, though on a smaller scale, only reinforced Palestinian determination to reject Israel's legitimacy.

Rejection of Israel, however, was not enough; the plight of the Palestinians living in refugee camps and in diaspora required a solution. At first Palestinians sought this solution through the achievement of Arab unity, but the failure of the Arab countries to unite and the military defeat of the regular Arab armies in 1967 led, among other factors, to disillusionment with Arab nationalist leaders and programs. After 1968 the PNC resolutions voiced a more specifically Palestinian nationalism, both as an affirmation of Palestinian existence in the face of Israeli denials and as a reflection of changes in the PNC constituency. New, radicalized groups entered the arena who criticized the Arab governments and demanded autonomy from them. Also, the balance between diaspora Palestinians and those living under Israeli occupation changed when Israel conquered the West Bank and Gaza. The more independent and politically diverse PNCs produced the more innovative resolutions of the second phase. They accepted the presence of the immigrant Jewish community in Palestine but rejected the Zionist denial of the Palestinian Arabs' right to self-determination.

In the wake of the 1973 war the PNC debates became increasingly pragmatic. Recognizing that the ideal of a single secular, non-discriminatory state for both peoples had little chance of realization, the Palestinians devoted increasing attention to the two-state solution. They first called for the establishment of a national "authority" on any part of Palestinian soil that was liberated, as an interim stage; subsequently they broached the respective principles of a Palestinian "entity" and a Palestinian state which, they implied, would be bounded by the cease-fire lines of 1967. Then they supported the Arab Summit's Fez plan (1982), which called for an independent Palestinian state in the West Bank and Gaza and for international guarantees of all the states in the area. This implicit adoption of the two-state solution was spelled out more and more explicitly in successive PNCs. By the time that the latest, Nineteenth, PNC was concluded the two-state solution had become its official policy, and the PLO was explicitly and unambiguously in favor of the principle that all states in the region, including Israel, had the right to security and sovereignty, in accord with the resolutions of the United Nations.

Concurrently, there was a significant evolution with regard to the means for achieving this goal. Starting in 1975 diplomatic means were mentioned alongside "armed struggle" as ways for realizing Palestinian national aspirations, and with the passage of time diplomatic efforts were given more prominence. Thus in 1984 the Seventeenth PNC called the convening of an international conference "the appropriate framework" for reaching a solution to the conflict. A peaceful, diplomatic resolution, based on UN Resolutions 181, 242, 338 and others, is now the heart of PNC policy.

At a time when Israeli hard-liners are openly advocating the expulsion of all Palestinians remaining in Israel proper and in the occupied territories, the moderation of the Palestinians is especially noteworthy. As the PNC resolutions demonstrate, this moderation is the product of lengthy debate and hard-won consensus. In its most developed form, expressed in Yasir Arafat's statements of 14 December 1988, the position adopted by the PNC represents a sound basis for a negotiated settlement of the Palestinian/Israeli conflict.

Toward Coexistence: An Analysis of the Resolutions of the Palestine National Council

Muhammad Muslih

When on 14 December 1988 Yasir Arafat recognized Israel, accepted UN Security Council Resolution 242, and renounced terrorism, leading the U.S. to open a dialogue with the Palestine Liberation Organization (PLO), the media were abuzz with speculation concerning his motives. Even commentators who pointed out that Arafat was in fact restating the PLO decisions taken a month earlier at the Nineteenth Palestine National Council (PNC) in Algiers often suggested that the "shift" was too abrupt to be credible, that it was a tactic aimed at securing the dialogue rather than a reflection of true policy. The fact that the Palestine National Charter of 1968 had not been formally renounced was repeatedly cited as evidence that, whatever public postures may be adopted, the PLO and its leaders remained at bottom committed to Israel's destruction. This evaluation continues to dominate official Israeli thinking and still appears fre-

---

The author wishes to thank Linda Butler for her major editorial assistance and revisions.

quently on the editorial pages of major U.S. newspapers.

In fact, the momentous decisions taken at the Nineteenth PNC, which enabled Arafat to pursue his course of action, were the product of a gradual evolution that had been taking place over many years. There should be no need for speculation here, for the organization's long march to the two-state solution definitively embraced in Algiers is a matter of public record, spelled out in a continuous chain of resolutions, extending over a period of two decades, that had been formulated at successive PNCs subsequent to the promulgation of the National Charter of 1964 and the amended National Charter of 1968. The documents issued by the PNCs—both the Charters and the resolutions—represent the official policy of the PLO and hence of the Palestinian people. An analysis of these texts thus reveals the unfolding changes in Palestinian political thinking.

* * *

Given the increasing—if in some quarters grudging—acceptance of the PLO's representativity of the Palestinian people, it might seem unnecessary to dwell on this issue unduly. Nonetheless, a few words may be in order. The available evidence indicates that the organization enjoys strong societal support and that it articulates political demands endorsed by a large majority of the Palestinian people. This has been borne out by every poll, formal and informal, carried out in the occupied territories: a major poll conducted by the Jerusalem weekly *al-Fajr* and the American newspaper *Newsday* in 1986, for example, showed that a full 93.5 percent of the West Bank and Gaza Palestinians supported the PLO and that 78.8 percent supported PLO chairman Yasir Arafat.[1] Since the beginning of the intifada in December 1987, both the Unified National Command of the Uprising (UNCU) and the political leaders in the West Bank and Gaza have repeatedly stressed their loyalty to the organization. Internationally, more than 100 states formally recognize the PLO as the legitimate representative of the Palestinian people. The United States implicitly subscribed to this when it opened the dialogue in December 1988, and State Department officials have frequently recognized informally that the PLO represents the Palestinian people. Even Israeli Military Intelligence conceded this fact in a report published in March 1989.[2]

The PLO derives its popular support and legitimacy from its struggle to attain the national political rights of the Palestinian people and from its role as the articulator of Palestinian nationalism. Of immense importance, too, have been the cultural, social, and economic services it has rendered to the Palestinians of the diaspora. Working through a multiplicity of organizational sub-units, both political and service-oriented, the PLO has made great efforts to rebuild a society that had been shattered politically, culturally, and economically. Indeed, a large part of the PLO's resources over the years has been devoted not to military activities but to creating a vast network of socioeconomic organizations.[3]

The PLO has been virtually synonymous with Palestinian nationalism since at least 1969, when effective control of the organization passed from the Arab states, under whose Arab League auspices it had been created in 1964, to the Palestinians themselves, and more particularly to the founders of Fateh who have comprised the core of its leadership ever since. But even before this important change gave the organization autonomy of decision, the PLO was the only body that could claim to represent the Palestinian people at large. As such, it enjoyed wide support even during the pre-1969 period, despite its shortcomings.

The PNC

The Palestine National Council is the highest body of the PLO. As the PLO's quasi-parliament, it defines the organization's policies and programs; indeed, it was the PNC which in effect created the PLO when it adopted at its first meeting in May-June 1964 the Fundamental Law, or statutes, setting out the distribution of powers among the various bodies of the PLO.

Since its first session in 1964, the PNC has gone through a number of changes in terms of composition and functions. According to the PLO's Fundamental Law, the Council in principle is to meet once a year, though this has not been strictly observed; it may also hold emergency sessions when it deems necessary. Because of the geographical dispersal of the Palestinians and the restrictive political environments in which they operate, elections to the quasi-parliament have never been held, but the membership represents a broad cross section of the Palestinian people living in the diaspora as well as under Israeli occupation. Membership has ranged from 150 to over 400; at present, it includes about 410 members. Since 1969, when political power in the PLO became concentrated in the hands of the political-commando organizations, the PNC membership has represented the proportional strength of these organizations as well as of the various mass movements and associations (trade unions, women's, teachers', and students' associations, various professional unions, etc.) It also reflects the relative size of the Palestinian communities in the diaspora and includes large numbers of "independents," or Palestinians not affiliated with any of the political-commando organizations. Fateh has always had more delegates to the PNC than any other group except the independents owing to its political and military preponderance. And because many independents favor Fateh's more centrist and non-ideological approach, they tend to shift the balance of forces even more decisively in Fateh's—and Arafat's—favor. It is for this reason that the smaller leftist/Marxist organizations such as the Popular Front for the Liberation of Palestine (PFLP), the Democratic Front for the Liberation of Palestine (DFLP), the pro-Syrian Sa'iqah, and so on, have been unable to constitute an effective counterweight to the Fateh/independent coalition. Not only are their constituencies much smaller than Fateh's, but the political differences among them tend to keep them at odds with each other and even to force some of them to side with Fateh in return for political protection.

* * *

Because of the constraints imposed by the dispersal of the Palestinian people and the absence of a territorially based central authority, there is no alternative to the PNC. It is the only Palestinian body in which the politics of consensus on a pluralistic basis prevails. Given the very nature of the PNC, the political resolutions (or programs) it formulates are the result of intense debate and consultation among the delegates and represent the widest common denominator among the Palestinians, including diverse PLO groups.

Moreover, while the political resolutions of the PNC are addressed both to the Palestinian people and to the outside world, they are by no means propaganda either for Western or for domestic Palestinian consumption. Rather, they are a frank expression of the PLO's inner dialogue and thus an important barometer of the actual thinking of the Palestinian movement.

PNC resolutions are binding on the PLO Executive Committee—which is elected by the PNC and which functions as the Palestinian movement's cabinet—until the subsequent PNC meeting issues new resolutions that may amend and supersede those hitherto in force. Thus, once adopted, the resolutions become a point of reference and a legitimizing instrument for policies pursued by the PLO leadership, as was the case when Arafat referred to the Nineteenth PNC as the basis for his declarations in Geneva in December 1988.

The focus of this study will be the political resolutions of the PNC that deal with overall Palestinian strategy vis-à-vis the core conflict. Nonetheless, it should be noted that the PNC deliberations and resolutions cover the broad spectrum of Palestinian concerns: the political resolutions per se generally account for no more than forty to fifty percent of the resolutions as a whole, the others addressing social, cultural, military, and other matters. Moreover, a large body of the political resolutions themselves addresses tactical matters relating to the immediate conjuncture of forces and events, that is, with the facts on the ground. Thus, an examination of the political resolutions over the years yields an account of the vicissitudes of PLO relations in Jordan, the evolving situation in Lebanon, the organization's changing ties with Egypt, the fallout from the 1983 rebellion within Fateh, and so on. Many of the resolutions that concern such crises will be left out of this account, and the tactical issues reflecting changing relations with various Arab states will be dealt with here primarily insofar as they have direct bearing on the movement's overall strategy and the means adopted to further it.

Before proceeding further, a word should be said about the relationship between the PNC resolutions and the National Charters of 1964 and 1968—all documents formulated and adopted by the PNC. The 1968 National Charter, which clearly supersedes that of 1964, formulates Palestinian rights in *optimal* terms. It is at once legalistic, utopian, and ideological, a kind of manifesto of Palestinian beliefs and what the Palestinian movement wanted to achieve in the past. The resolutions, on the other hand, are a formulation of the *program of action* in the light of the realities on the ground—local, regional, and international. From the legal standpoint, the resolutions do not supersede the Charter and cannot of themselves rescind it. But in practice, they cumulatively reveal the unmistakable trend away from the maximalist, utopian terms of the National Charter towards an evolving cognizance of what is possible and what is not. With successive PNCs, the gap between the theoretical and the action-policies of the PLO continued to grow. By the time of the Nineteenth PNC in November 1988 in Algiers, the National Charter was to all intents and purposes, though not in specific terms, rescinded, if only because of the diametrical opposition between the basic premises of the Declaration of Independence (e.g., the partition of Palestine as the objective and peaceful negotiation as the means of achieving it) and the basic premises of the National Charter (e.g., the total liberation of Palestine as the objective and armed struggle as the exclusive means of achieving it). In essence, then, Arafat was correct when, during his visit to Paris in May 1989, he pronounced the National Charter *"caduc,"* or "lapsed," though in the formal sense it is still operative.

Technically speaking, for the Charter to be amended, two-thirds of the PNC members must vote to do so in a special session convened especially for this purpose. The Palestinian leadership believes that it has given all the concessions in this regard that it can give without reciprocity from the Israeli government. The implication is that the Charter will be legally amended or altogether rescinded within the context of a final Israeli/Palestinian settlement.

* * *

On the basis of a careful and sequential reading of the political resolutions of PNCs One through Nineteen, with particular reference to *objectives* and *means*, three major stages can be identified which provide a convenient framework for discussion. These are as follows: (1) the "total liberation" phase, from 1964 through 1968; (2) the secular democratic state phase, from 1969 through 1973; and (3) the two-state solution phase. This last itself underwent a gradual but steady evolution, beginning somewhat tentatively in 1974 and culminating in the explicitly spelled-out acceptance of a Palestinian state alongside Israel not as a transitional stage but as a *point final*. This evolution in the framing of goals parallels an evolution in the specification of the *means* of achieving them, from exclusive reliance on armed struggle, to partial reliance on diplomacy in conjunction with armed struggle, to equal reliance on the two, to the elevation of diplomatic effort at the expense of military effort (including direct contact with Israeli groups and individuals), to insistence on participation in a Middle East peace conference and readiness to open a direct dialogue with the Israeli government.

The Total Liberation Phase: The First Four PNCs

During the first four years of the PLO's existence, from its creation in 1964 through 1968, the Palestinian movement remained totally under the impact of what the Palestinians call *al-Nakba*—the Catastrophe—the creation of Israel by force of arms in about 77 percent of what had been Palestine, and the displacement of some two thirds of the Palestinian people to Transjordan, Syria, Lebanon, the Egyptian-administered Gaza Strip, and the West Bank later annexed by Transjordan.

The Palestinians' overriding preoccupation with what had befallen them is clearly reflected in the two documents that dominate this phase—the National Charter of 1964, formulated by the First PNC, and the amended National Charter of 1968, drawn up by the Fourth PNC, as well as in the resolutions of the Second and Third PNCs that came in between. All of these documents emphasize the *total liberation* of Palestine, "the recovery of the usurped homeland *in its entirety*" (preamble of the 1964 Charter; emphasis added). Palestine is defined within the "boundaries which existed during the British Mandate"; it "consti-

9

tutes *an indivisible territorial unit*" (article 2 of the 1964 and 1968 Charters; emphasis added). Palestinian insistence on total liberation was mandated not only by the sense of injustice concerning what had happened, but, more pragmatically, by the fact that the overwhelming majority of the Palestinians lived in the diaspora, thus requiring a solution that would permit their return to their lands. During this phase, then, any suggestion of the partition of Palestine (declared "null and void" in article 17 of the 1964 Charter and in article 19 of the 1968 Charter) is summarily rejected. Thus, when Tunisian President Habib Bourguiba proposed in 1965 that the Palestinians accept partition as "a lesser evil" than the evil of dispossession, he was branded with "high treason against the Palestinian cause" (resolution 1.A of the Second PNC).

The 1964 and 1968 National Charters, which bracket this phase, are continually depicted as aggressive documents, yet in Palestinian eyes they were defensive. This is explicitly stated: "the liberation of Palestine is a defensive act necessitated by the requirements of self-defense" as prescribed in the charter of the United Nations (articles 16 and 18 in the 1964 and 1968 Charters, respectively). For the Palestinians, the National Charters were a response to the ideological premises of Zionism deriving from the Basle program of 1897, which they perceived as the delegitimization of Palestinian rights in Palestine. For them, Zionism was "aggressive and expansionist in its goals," a "constant source of threat," an "imperialist invasion" that led to the creation of Israel at the expense of the Palestinians; indeed, given the facts of demography and land ownership in Palestine prior to 1948, one can say without risk of misstatement that the dispossession and eviction of the Palestinian people was the *sine qua non* for the creation and development of the Jewish state.[4] Repeated references to the Palestinians' "right" to recover their land or to return to it likewise indicate this defensive nature. Contrary to the assertions of some commentators, it is not vengeance and hatred that characterizes the documents, but an enormous sense of loss: surely there is a different nuance in calling for "liberation of the homeland," "recovery of the land"—phrases that recur repeatedly throughout both Charters—and the oft-cited call for the "destruction of Israel," which in fact appears nowhere in either text. What one does find are three statements, all in the amended National Charter of 1968: that the Arabs must "repel the Zionist and imperialist invasion from the greater Arab homeland and liquidate the Zionist presence in Palestine" (article 15), that the elimination of "the Zionist and imperialist presence in the country [would] lead to the establishment of peace in the Middle East" (article 22), and that the "requirements of right and justice require all nations . . . to consider Zionism an illegal movement and to outlaw its presence and activities" (article 23). These statements show an unquestionable escalation in the National Charter of 1968 vis-à-vis that of 1964, an escalation not unrelated to the fact that the amended document was adopted in the wake of the conquest of the remaining 23 percent of Palestinian territory and the expulsion across the Jordan of a further 250,000 refugees.

It should be noted as well that there are no calls for the elimination of Jews, although both Charters state that the Jews are not "one people having an independent identity. They are rather citizens of the countries to which they belong" (articles 18 and 20 of the 1964 and 1968 Charters, respectively). Concerning the position of Jews in the Palestine to be liberated, the 1964 Charter stipulates that "Jews who are of Palestinian origin shall be considered Palestinians if they are willing to live peacefully and loyally in Palestine" (article 7), "Palestinian" being defined in article 6 as those who "normally resided in Palestine until 1947." The 1968 Charter, written after the 1967 war had brought what remained of historic Palestine under Israeli control, shows a regression in this regard; article 6 states that "the Jews who had resided normally in Palestine *until the beginning of the Zionist invasion* shall be considered Palestinians" (emphasis added).

It has been suggested that this first phase represents in essence a rejection of history, an effort to turn back the clock—a charge which Zionists would be hard pressed to claim as an exclusively Palestinian preoccupation. Notwithstanding, the Palestinians during this first phase wanted to "restore the legitimate situation to Palestine" (article 16, 1964 Charter); "The Balfour Declaration and the instrument of the Mandate, with all their attending consequences, are null and void" (article 18, 1964 Charter; article 20, 1968 Charter). The partitioning of Palestine and the establishment of Israel are likewise declared null and void (articles 17 and 19 in Charters 1964 and 1968, respectively). To an extent, then, this phase represents an exercise in wishful thinking, an outright rejection of the present reality and a refusal to work within it. It is a call for the restoration of the status quo ante, in which, were the usual norms of proportional representation observed, the Palestinians would automatically recover their legitimate rights, including their right to self-determination.

* * *

The first four PNCs show a great unity regarding objectives, all being centered on the total liberation of Palestine, but an important shift in *means* occurs as of the Fourth PNC. Whereas the first three imply that the conventional Arab armies are the instrument of liberation, the Fourth not only adopts the principle of armed struggle but shifts the agent of liberation away from the Arab states to the Palestinians themselves.

In fact, the 1964 National Charter and the resolutions of the Second and Third PNCs include few specific directives as to how the liberation of Palestine is to be achieved: only three of the twenty-nine articles in the 1964 Charter contain any reference to means at all, and then only in the vaguest terms. Article 12 states that "Arab unity and the liberation of Palestine are two complementary goals: each prepares the way for the attainment of the other." Article 13 says the Palestinian people shall play the "vanguard role in the realization of this sacred national goal," and article 14 stipulates that the liberation of Palestine is a "national duty, full responsibility for which rests upon the entire Arab nation" which must "mobilize all its military, material, and spiritual resources in order to liberate Palestine." These same ideas are echoed in the Second and Third PNCs, although the Third is slightly more explicit, declaring that the liberation of Palestine can only be achieved through military engagement (resolution l).

With the Fourth PNC, however, the means become not merely explicit but a central part of the program. Article 9 of the 1968 National Charter stipulates that *"armed struggle is the only way to liberate Palestine"* (emphasis added). The Palestinians are called upon to "work for an armed popular revolution for the liberation of their country and their return to it." Article 10 states that "commando action constitutes the nucleus of the Palestinian popular war of liberation." The concept of armed struggle recurs more than ten times in the 1968 Charter in an emphatic and uncompromising tone. Meanwhile, the new stress on Palestinian self-reliance is reflected in the fact that the principles of Palestinian self-determination and national sovereignty over a totally liberated Palestine is underscored at least eight times in the 1968 Charter, and in the use of the word "Palestinian" rather than "Arab": the "Arab homeland" of the 1964 Charter, for example, becomes in 1968 the "homeland of the Palestinian Arab people." It is true that the 1968 Charter still carries many references to Arab unity and cooperation, but the emphasis is different. Article 12 states, for example: "The Palestinian Arab people believe in Arab unity. In order to play their role in attaining it, *they must, at this stage of their national struggle, preserve their Palestinian identity and its components*. They must also strengthen their self-awareness, and oppose all schemes that may dissolve or weaken their identity" (emphasis added). Palestinian self-reliance thus becomes a means to an end.

The escalation in revolutionary language and the primacy ascribed to armed struggle in the amended National Charter adopted by the Fourth PNC was determined by two interrelated factors: the strategically relevant political developments, and the institutional changes within the PLO. Indeed, the Fourth PNC was held just over a year after the crushing defeat of the Arab armies in the 1967 war discredited conventional warfare as the means of liberating Palestine. At the same time, the 1967 debacle gave new credibility to the concept of guerrilla warfare called for by the commando organizations,[5] which had been challenging the PLO leadership since the mid-1960s. It was only a matter of time before they would gain ascendancy within the organization.

The PLO, as mentioned earlier, had been set up by the Arab states under the auspices of the Arab League in what could be seen as a somewhat cynical move aimed less at fighting Israel than at creating a facade behind which their own inaction would be effectively concealed.[6] Hence their aversion to any activity that could lead to confrontation with Israel and threaten the regional status quo. This orientation was enhanced by the PLO's first leadership under Ahmad al-Shuqayri, carefully handpicked by Egyptian President Gamal Abd al-Nasir. Shuqayri was a conservative of upper class origins with long experience in the power centers of the status-quo oriented Arab states, and most of the other PLO leaders were of similar backgrounds. The absence of armed struggle from the 1964 Charter and the resolutions of the first three PNCs, as well as the fact that article 24 of the 1964 Charter stated that the PLO would not have any administrative control over the West Bank and Gaza, show the extent of the PLO's readiness in those days to defer to Arab official demands and wishes.

The growing influence of Fateh had begun to challenge the PLO leadership as of the Second PNC in May 1965, when it used that forum to criticize the organization's lack of "revolutionary zeal." By the time the Third PNC was held a year later, guerrilla actions against Israel were proving an embarrassment to what the commando organizations called the "fighters inside offices" of the PLO. The statement in the Third PNC's political program that "freedom of Palestinian action is a *sine qua non* for waging the battle of liberation" (Ii) reflects the influence of the commando movement even then, as does the the reference, for the first time, to "revolutionary" groups, action, and leadership. With the debacle of the June 1967 war, Shuqayri's personalized and uncreative rule was totally discredited. At the Fourth PNC in July 1968, the commando organizations were represented for the first time. With Fateh holding half the seats in the new Council, they gained control of the organization.

The new leadership, dominated by Fateh's inner circle that had coalesced in the late 1950s out of student organizations in Cairo and Kuwait, argued for Palestinian self-reliance and independence from the Arab regimes. The newly constituted PLO that emerged from the Fourth PNC stressed the need to build the sociopolitical institutions of a reinvigorated Palestinian national movement. On another front, it sought to escalate the strategy of armed struggle by planning for a popular uprising within the occupied territories and by launching guerrilla attacks from Lebanon and across Israel's new frontiers along the Jordan.[7] The strategy of self-reliance and the language of revolution and armed struggle adopted by the organization at a time when the Arab governments had come to see the need for a diplomatic settlement go a long way toward explaining the Palestinian encounter with the Jordanian army in 1970/71 and the Syrian army in 1976 and 1983. But by the same token, the continuity of its leadership—which has remained in place to this day—strengthened its ability to survive the overwhelming assaults of external foes bent on its destruction.

The triumph of the guerrilla organizations led by Fateh was due not merely to the appeal among the Palestinian masses of the strategy of armed struggle following the defeat of the Arab armies. Fateh's Palestinian nationalism carried the day because it was in keeping with the far-reaching changes that swept the entire Arab world as a result of the 1967 debacle: pan-Arabism as the ideology that for well over a decade had been virtually the defining characteristic of Arab and Palestinian politics was in retreat; the state system was being consolidated. Most Palestinians had wholeheartedly subscribed to the pan-Arabist proposition that Arab unity was the road to the liberation of Palestine. They had spontaneously entrusted their cause to the Arab leaders, particularly Egyptian president Gamal Abd al-Nasir. The 1967 war had proved them wrong. With the Fourth PNC, the ascendancy of Palestinian nationalism was complete, with all that implied in terms of strategy and tactics.

The Secular Democratic State Phase: The Fifth through Eleventh PNCs

The second phase, from 1969 through 1973, was characterized by a shift of objective. While the liberation of all Palestine remained the ultimate goal, the vision of the state that was to emerge from liberation underwent a significant change, from a primarily Arab state to one that would be shared with *all* Jews resident in Palestine if they renounced Zionism. There was no longer any stipulation, as there had been in the two National Charters, concerning the Jews' length of residence in Palestine. Thus, the Fifth PNC in February

1969 introduced for the first time in a collective, official Palestinian document the idea of establishing a "free democratic society in Palestine encompassing all Palestinians, including Muslims, Christians, and Jews... and rescuing Palestine from the hegemony of International Zionism." Seven months later, the Sixth PNC reiterated the same idea but replaced the term "society" with that of "state." The other PNCs of the period elaborated on the idea: the Eighth (February/March 1971), for example, specified that "all those who wish to live in peace shall enjoy the same rights and duties," while the Eleventh (January 1973) called for the establishment of a "democratic society" where "all citizens... can live in equality, justice and fraternity" and which would be "opposed to all forms of prejudice on the basis of race, color, and creed." Thus, the concept of the secular democratic state provided a clear answer to the question of the future of the Jews in a liberated Palestine and eliminated the earlier ambiguity that surrounded this issue.

To understand the strategy behind the adoption of the secular state idea, it must be recalled that the PLO was a national movement whose adherents lived primarily in exile. The diaspora Palestinians—a large portion of the Palestinian people as a whole—had their homes and roots in the three-quarters of Palestine that was captured by the Jewish forces in 1948 and thus felt they had little to gain from anything less than a total return. But the Palestine of 1969 was not the same as the Palestine of 1948, and a formula had to be found for dealing with the Jewish population that was there. The concept of a non-sectarian, democratic state was the PLO's answer to this challenge. From today's perspective, the democratic state could appear extremist and maximalist, but to the Palestinians at the time it represented a formidable concession. For the first time, they declared themselves prepared to *share* their homeland, which they considered to be wholly theirs by *right*, with the Jews, the vast majority of whom had come recently to Palestine as immigrants and who were perceived to have displaced them. Moreover, by adopting the concept of a secular democratic state, the Palestinians were attempting in their own fashion to reach out to all the Jews who were by that time already established on Palestinian soil.

In line with this phase's twin goals of total liberation and the establishment of a secular, democratic state on all of Palestine, "partial" or "capitulationist solutions" continued to be vigorously rejected. These included UN Security Council Resolution 242, the Soviet peace plan of December 1969 (which was based on 242 and which called for a phased Israeli withdrawal from the territories occupied in 1967 and for a "just solution of the refugee problem") and the Rogers Plan of December 1969 (likewise based on the land-for-peace formula embodied in 242). All these were summarily rejected at the emergency session of August 1970 on the grounds that they entailed "recognition of the legitimacy of the occupying enemy." Yet another plan, King Hussein's "United Arab Kingdom Plan" unveiled in March 1972, proposed the creation of a federated state on both banks of the Jordan in the event that Israel withdrew from the occupied territories. The Tenth PNC was convened the following month specifically to counter it.

Similarly, there was uncompromising rejection of the idea of establishing a Palestinian state on Palestinian territory occupied by Israel in 1967. In the political programs of the emergency session of August 1970 (which condemned any "partitioning of the country"), as well as of the Eighth (February/March 1971), Ninth (July 1971), and Eleventh (January 1973) sessions, the word used to describe such a state was *duwaylah* (ministate), a diminutive form of *dawlah* (state) that is in itself disparaging. There is no doubt that this position was in harmony with the prevailing political preference of the Palestinians at the time. When the well-known Egyptian writer and journalist Ahmad Baha' al-Din proposed the creation of a Palestinian state in the occupied territories in late 1967, his call received no support from the Palestinians.[8] Some considered the suggestion premature, in view of the fact that neither the Palestinians nor the Arab states were yet ready for such a step. The more pressing goal was the "elimination of the consequences of aggression," otherwise stated, the return to Arab sovereignty of the Arab lands conquered by Israel in June 1967.

The secular democratic state remained the goal of the PLO until 1974, when the organization made its first steps towards the two-state solution at the Twelfth PNC. Even then, the secular democratic state was not clearly and explicitly renounced, and some continued to cherish it as an ideal, a "noble dream"—which in fact is how Arafat characterized it as early as November 1974 in his speech to the United Nations General Assembly. In that speech, which reinforced the movement away from the democratic secular state as a programmatic objective already foreshadowed in the Twelfth PNC, he also made clear that the realization of this "dream" was contingent upon Jewish consent and cooperation. It is in this form that the secular democratic state idea has survived to the present in some circles—as a kind of utopic vision not at odds with the two-state solution but which looks to a day when Israel and an eventual Palestinian state would decide to merge through a process of *mutual consent*. Even for its adherents, then, it has ceased to be a programmatic "goal" in the concrete sense it had been during the PLO's secular democratic state phase and has been relegated to the status of a "preferred outcome" that may or may not be realizable.

* * *

In the late sixties and early seventies, of course, the democratic secular state was the concrete goal set by the PLO. With respect to the *means* posited for achieving it, the PNCs of this second phase maintained the emphasis on "armed struggle" and "popular war." There was, however, a vague reference to "other forms of struggle" in the Sixth PNC program. And in the Eighth PNC program (February/March 1971), armed struggle was posited as the *"principal* form of struggle for the liberation of Palestine" (emphasis added). This subtle change, the use of "principal" instead of "sole", contained the seeds of the PLO's embrace of diplomacy in the phase to come.

Meanwhile, disagreement over means between the mainstream Fateh and the more radical movements such as George Habash's PFLP and Nayef Hawatmeh's DFLP became acute during this period. These organizations, frustrated by the limits imposed on their activities by the Arab host countries, began to believe that the only solution to the dilemma was a popular revolution that would overthrow the existing Arab regimes and replace them with ones sympathetic to the Palestinian revolution: hence, George Habash's famous slogan to the effect that "the road to the liberation of Palestine runs through Amman." This stance inevitably led to an escalating confrontation, notably with Jordan, in which Fateh was somewhat reluctantly dragged along. With increasing calls by the radical groups for the "liberation of Jordan" from the "Hashemite regime that was in collusion with Israel," the situation between the PLO and Jordan deteriorated dramatically, culminating in King Hussein's liquidation of the commando presence in Jordan in 1970–71 and in his United Arab Kingdom Plan the following year which effectively ignored the PLO. This conflict occupied a prominent place in PNC sessions six through eleven, with the language of the resolutions concerning Hussein esclating to the Final Communique of the Tenth PNC in April 1972, which went beyond the usual attacks and actually called for his overthrow.*

It should be noted that although this secular democratic state phase was consistent in its rejection of a Palestinian state in only part of Palestinian territory, there was at the very end of this phase an unprecedented interest shown in the occupied territories. Thus, the political program of the Eleventh PNC (January 1973) shows a noticeable increase in the PLO's involvement in the politics of the West Bank and Gaza. Almost the entire first section of the program, "In the

---

*Henry Kissinger claimed in his memoirs that the PLO went so far as to solicit U.S. support in its attempt to overthrow King Hussein, first approaching the American government in mid-1973, and reiterating the position in a secret meeting with an official U.S. representative in Rabat, Morocco, in November of that year. See Henry Kissinger, *Years of Upheaval* (Boston: Little, Brown, and Co., 1982), pp. 624–29.

Palestinian Arena," was taken up with the need to adopt concrete measures to "mobilize the masses" in the West Bank and Gaza and to build up economic and cultural institutions that would enhance the people's ability "to stay put on the land" (section I.7). It was in the spirit of this PNC that the Palestine National Front was established in the summer of 1973 with the express purpose of coordinating and spearheading nationalist resistance in the occupied territories[9]—a role it played with significant success until the late 1970s. This new emphasis was to prove significant, and unfolded with more coherence in the following phase, thus signalling the PLO's movement towards accommodating the political priorities of its constituency in the occupied territories. Ultimately, this development had a profound impact on the overall strategy of the PLO.

The Two-State Solution Phase (The Twelfth through Nineteenth PNCs, June 1974 to November 1988)

It was in July of 1974, less than a year after the October 1973 war opened new hopes for a comprehensive Middle East settlement, that the PLO embarked irrevocably on the road towards pragmatism that culminated in the November 1988 Declaration of a Palestinian state in the occupied territories and the definitive acceptance of a two-state solution. The years between were marked by far-reaching events—the Lebanese civil war, Sadat's visit to Jerusalem, the Camp David accords, the Israeli-Egyptian separate peace, the 1982 Israeli invasion of Lebanon, the outbreak of the intifada. These events were accompanied by the ebb and flow of the Palestinian movement—the formation of the Rejection Front and the PFLP's temporary withdrawal from the PLO Executive Committee, a hardening of attitudes following the Sadat visit, the rebellion and defection of the Abu Musa faction of Fateh in 1983, and so on. But throughout this long and complex period, the march towards the two-state solution was relatively stable and steady.

The Twelfth PNC in June 1974 marked a turning point of major significance in Palestinian political thought. It was this council that issued the ten-point program first calling for the establishment of the "people's national, independent, and fighting authority on every part of Palestinian land to be liberated." It is true that the resolution made no mention of a "state" but only of the vague concept of an "authority." It is also true that the resolution specified that the "people's national authority" was a transitional stage, and that the ultimate goal remained unchanged. Thus, point 4 of the program stated that "any liberation step taken is taken in the pursuit of the *realization of the PLO strategy for the establishment of the Palestinian democratic state* as stipulated in the previous resolutions of the PNC" (emphasis added), while point 8 noted that "the Palestinian national authority, after its establishment, shall struggle for the unity of the front-line states for the sake of *completing the liberation of all Palestinian soil*. . ." (emphasis added). Point 3, meanwhile, reiterates that the "PLO shall struggle against any plan for the establishment of a Palestinian entity, the price of which is recognition, conciliation, secure borders, renunciation of national rights. . . ."

Still, even with these qualifiers, the Twelfth PNC represents a remarkable break with the past, given the repeated and vociferous rejections of the "ministate" and the principle of partition, even as an interim stage, in earlier PNCs. The Twelfth PNC thus set the stage for far-reaching changes in the years that lay ahead, initiating the policy shift towards coexistence with Israel. The change was halting and cautious, the language heralding it often ambiguous in the interests of achieving consensus among the disparate groups forming the PLO. Indeed, the programs of PNCs Twelve through Eighteen can be described as programs of creative ambiguity, with the degree of vagueness concerning ultimate objectives diminishing gradually, but not altogether disappearing, until the Nineteenth program in November 1988.

A number of factors contributed to the elaboration of the ministate idea that was introduced in germ form in the Twelfth PNC. The need for the Palestinians to stake a clear claim to the occupied territories was brought home by King Hussein's March 1972 announcement of the United Arab Kingdom plan comprising the East and West Banks of the Jordan River in the event of Israeli withdrawal. Moreover, by 1974, there was widespread recognition among the Palestinian leadership that whatever the intellectual and emotional appeal the democratic secular state idea might enjoy in some quarters, it had received little political support from either the most pro-Palestinian Israeli circles, or internationally from the traditional supporters of the Palestinian movement.

The idea of a ministate in the occupied territories was also a nod to the wishes of the West Bank and Gaza Palestinians who strongly supported it and who were becoming an increasingly important part of the PLO constituency.[10] At the same time, the tentativeness in the language of the resolution (the use of the word "authority" rather than "state") and the addition of the hawkish term "fighting" to modify "authority" were intended to enable the PLO hardliners, who were not ready to concede even a square inch of Palestinian territory, to subscribe to the resolutions. The program was in fact adopted by all the commando groups, including the PFLP, the PFLP-General Command, the Arab Liberation Front (ALF), and the DFLP. But although these groups adopted the resolution, they subsequently formed the "Rejection Front" on the grounds that the ministate would lead to an abandonment of armed struggle and to coexistence with Israel.

Neither the formation of the Rejection Front nor the PFLP's withdrawal in protest from the PLO Executive Committee in September 1974 led to any retreat from the position articulated at the Twelfth PNC session, however. On the contrary, the Thirteenth PNC in March 1977 went even further than the Twelfth: the call for an "independent national state on their own land" (point 11) became explicit, albeit with the proviso that there could be no state at the "expense of our people's inalienable rights" (point 4). Moreover, for the first time since 1968 there was not a single reference to "total liberation." Nor did the return of Habash's PFLP (which had boycotted the Thirteenth PNC) to the Fourteenth PNC as a result of the closing of ranks following Sadat's trip to Jerusalem and the signing of the Camp David accords halt the trend. Thus, the Fourteenth PNC reaffirmed the 15-point program of the Thirteenth and emphasized the Palestinians' right to establish "their independent state on their soil," and the Fifteenth PNC (April 1981) called for "the establishment of their independent state on the soil of their homeland" under the leadership of the PLO.

Except for a passing mention in the Fourteenth PNC to the Palestinian right to a *democratic* state on the *whole* of their national soil (but note that the reference is to the "right" to such a state rather than a call for its realization), there was no further mention from this time forward either to total liberation or to the concept of a secular, democratic state. The absence of such references, together with the explicit endorsement of the UN resolutions relevant to the Palestine question in the Thirteenth, Fourteenth, and the Fifteenth PNCs, suggest a willingness to accept an independent Palestinian state in parts of Palestine.

A further indication of change in this phase is the PNC's treatment of UN Security Council Resolution 242. Earlier PNCs had repudiated the resolution in keeping with their rejection of "all solutions which do not postulate the total liberation of Palestine, and all proposals whose aim is the liquidation or internationalization of the Palestine cause" (1968 Charter). The Fifth PNC (February 1969), for example, explicitly rejected 242 as a *"peaceful* and capitulationist" solution that conflicts "with the full right of the Palestinian people to their homeland" (emphasis added), while the emergency session of August 1970 rejected it on the basis of its consequences, one of which would be "opening negotiations with the occupying imperialist Zionist enemy." As recently as the Eleventh PNC, Resolution 242 had been included among the "maneuvers and plots," "liquidationist plans," and "partial settlements" that "consecrate Zionist usurpation and lead to the liquidation of the Palestinian national cause." In contrast, the first clause of the Twelfth PNC rejects

27

242 only because it "obscures the national and pan-Arab rights of our people, and deals with the cause of our people as a refugee problem"—in other words, not because it embodied the principle of peaceful settlement or recognized Israel, but because it did not accommodate the political aspirations of the Palestinians. The Thirteenth through Eighteenth PNCs, when they explicitly rejected 242, did so in similar terms.

The PNC's evolving response to the various peace plans throughout this period provides further evidence of the PLO's growing readiness to come to terms with Israel. Thus, the Fifteenth PNC "welcomes" the February 1981 Brezhnev plan, which called for an all-party framework for a Middle East peace conference and for the establishment of a Palestinian state. The fact that the PNC welcomed a plan which not only stressed the need to "ensure the security and sovereignty of all states of the region, *including Israel*" (emphasis added) but further explicitly mentioned Israel's borders as the 1949–67 armistice lines[11] suggests a clear scaling back of Palestinian demands. By the Sixteenth PNC in February 1983, the "welcome" of the Soviet proposals had become "appreciation and support." The Sixteenth PNC also affirmed "its adherence to the ... principles of the UN charter, and resolutions which affirm the inalienable rights of the Palestinian people in order to establish a *just and comprehensive peace in the Middle East*" (emphasis added).

A similar evolution can be seen in the PNC's response to the Fez peace plan of September 1982, itself based on an earlier plan by Saudi Arabia's Crown Prince Fahd, from which the PLO leadership was not altogether alien. The Fez Plan called for the creation of a Palestinian state and for Israeli withdrawal from all the Arab territories occupied in 1967, so that while borders were not explicitly delineated a state limited to the West Bank and Gaza was clearly implied. The plan also called for international security guarantees and for recognizing "all states in the region" (an implicit recognition of Israel), and made favorable reference in its preamble to the 1965 Bourguiba plan advocating partition which had been so roundly condemned at the Second PNC.

When the Fez Plan was discussed at the Sixteenth PNC, the various organizations of the PLO were divided, with Fateh in favor and Sa'iqah, the PFLP, the PFLP-GC, and the Palestine Popular Struggle Front (PPSF) opposed. Arafat won over the DFLP and the PFLP, but because of the division the response of the Sixteenth PNC was muted: the Fez Plan was accepted merely as the "minimum for the political activity of the Arab states," which should be "complemented by military action . . . to rectify the balance of power in favor of struggle and of Palestinian and Arab rights." But even this less than wholehearted acceptance is significant, especially since all the factions, including the Rejection Front, participated in the Council and unity was maintained. By the time of the Eighteenth PNC in April 1987, the status of the Fez Plan had been elevated to that of a "framework for Arab action at the international level to achieve a solution to the Palestine question and to regain the occupied Arab territories." By accepting the Fez Plan as a framework for a solution to the Palestine question, the PLO was in effect accepting Israel and the two-state solution. The Reagan plan, on the other hand, was "rejected as a sound basis for a just and permanent solution of the Palestine question" because, among other reasons, "it denies the establishment of an independent Palestinian state."

Another important advance on the road to pragmatism was a new attitude towards Jordan starting with the Sixteenth PNC, the first to state clearly that "future relations with Jordan should be on the basis of a confederation between two independent states."[12] This idea was clearly an effort to address concerns about possible Palestinian radicalism even while preserving the independence and sovereignty of a future Palestinian state. It can be viewed as well as a concession both to Tel Aviv and Washington, given King Hussein's acceptability as a negotiating partner, and to Egypt, which had been encouraging the confederation idea and which had become a strategic PLO ally in the wake of Israel's invasion of Lebanon. The large Palestinian population in the East Bank, many with relatives and property in the occupied territories, was another factor in favor of endorsing confederation. At all events, the idea of confederation with Jordan was explicitly reiterated in all subsequent PNCs despite the collapse of the joint PLO-Jordanian initiative in February 1986.

* * *

Concerning the means of achieving the evolving goal of a Palestinian state alongside Israel, the phase that opened in 1974 with the Twelfth PNC is most accurately characterized by a decreasing emphasis on armed struggle and a correspondingly greater and more specific focus on diplomacy. Thus, while the Twelfth PNC mentions the PLO's readiness to "struggle by every means, foremost of which is armed struggle," subsequent sessions maintain armed struggle not as the guiding strategy but as an equal partner of diplomatic activity. Although virtually all the sessions affirm not merely the continuation of armed struggle, but even its "advancement" and "escalation against the Zionist occupation," starting from the Thirteenth PNC it is always mentioned "in conjunction with various forms of political and mass struggle" or alongside "all other forms of material and moral struggle." Moreover, no details or modalities are spelled out concerning armed struggle, whereas increasing space is devoted to the various other forms, notably diplomacy. Finally, during this period the word "struggle" is sometimes used without its modifying adjective "armed," leading some Palestinian critics to refer ironically to the "unarmed struggle" (*al-kifah al-mushallah*) that had come to characterize the movement.

Indeed, whatever lip service continued to be paid to armed struggle, it was clear that throughout this period diplomacy was the favored means for achieving Palestinian goals. In addition to the positive response to various peace plans recognizing Israel and providing for its security (such as the Brezhnev plan mentioned above), increasing attention was paid to strengthening relations with international forces in a position to help the Palestinian cause. Thus, the Fifteenth PNC stressed the importance of "securing wider recognition for the PLO . . . expressed its conviction that it is the right and duty of the Palestinian revolution to continue its political and diplomatic moves and activity at the international level, including the countries of Western Europe." Peace talks and the United Nations were likewise given more attention. Clause 15A of the Thirteenth PNC affirmed the "PLO's right to participate, independently and on an equal footing, in all international conferences, forums, and efforts relating to the Palestine question and the Arab-Zionist conflict." This point was reiterated and amplified in succeeding PNCs, until the Seventeenth specifically stated for the first time that the "appropriate framework" for a solution to the Palestine problem was "the convening of an international conference under the auspices of the United Nations, in consultation with the Security Council and others, and with the participation of all the concerned parties, on an equal footing, including the PLO. This conference must be held on the basis of UN resolutions relevant to the Palestine question." The Eighteenth PNC repeated this stance in slightly more detail, and to further its implementation endorsed "the proposal to form a preparatory committee or 'initiative committee.'" The Nineteenth PNC went even further; it dropped any reference to armed struggle, so that international diplomacy became the only publicly endorsed means for achieving Palestinian goals.

In line with Palestinian efforts to strengthen ties with international forces, the PNCs during this phase focused for the first time on relations with Jewish groups. Thus, the Thirteenth PNC clearly endorsed in clause 14 the idea of establishing ties and relations of coordination with "Jewish democratic and progressive forces . . . which are struggling against the ideology and practice of Zionism." By the Eighteenth PNC, ten years later, this formulation had become "enhancing relations with *Israeli* democratic forces that support the Palestinian people's struggle. . ." (emphasis added), and not simply with "Jewish forces" as in previous programs.[13]

Finally, the trend to place greater and more detailed

emphasis on the occupied territories as a central ingredient of PLO strategy and as an aspect of the movement towards the two-state solution intensified during this period. This emphasis, which became increasingly specific from the Thirteenth PNC on, was expressed in the form of support for the political work of the Palestine National Front in the occupied territories, support for various committees, trade unions, and economic projects, the establishment of a fund to support steadfastness, and other concrete financial and political measures.

* * *

Thus, from the Twelfth PNC in 1974 onwards, the Palestinians had been moving steadily towards accommodation and compromise. By the time the Eighteenth PNC was held in April 1987, most of the elements were in place: already contained in the PNC's embrace of the Fez Plan was implicit recognition of Israel, in effect an acceptance of the two-state solution. The desirability of confederation with Jordan of a Palestinian state was clearly spelled out; the preference for peaceful means in reaching a solution was manifest in the very specific call for an international conference under the auspices of the United Nations on the basis of UN resolutions relevant to the Palestine question. Yet the Council had stopped short of the explicit, unambiguous statement of these positions that had some chance of breaking the stalemate in the quest of Middle East peace.

This policy of moving ahead while holding back, of proposing vaguely and waiting for a response from the other side, became impossible with the events of 1987–88. The November 1987 Arab Summit conference in Amman came as a rude shock to the Palestinians, not only because of the somewhat offhanded treatment of Arafat at the hands of the Arab leaders but because, for the first time in Arab summit history, the Arab-Israeli conflict was virtually ignored. Not only, then, was the Palestine problem ignored in the international arena, it did not even command the attention of the Arab "brothers."

But although the summit brought home the need for an innovative Palestinian diplomatic initiative to reactivate the Palestinian case, the PLO would perhaps not have acted as decisively as it did had it not been for the outbreak of the intifada. Scarcely a month after the Amman summit, the uprising exploded all the equations of the situation and catapulted the priorities of the West Bank and Gaza Palestinians to the top of the PLO agenda: not to act would have risked losing influence in the occupied territories. King Hussein's disengagement from the West Bank the following July, by creating a political vacuum in the occupied territories that could invite Israeli annexation, further forced the PLO's hand. It was thus that, pressed by these external forces, the Palestinians were galvanized to cut through their internal ambiguities and to move definitively beyond the struggle between what they believed was *just* and what they realized was *possible*. The difficult task of making clearcut choices fell to the Palestine National Council convened for November 1988 in Algiers, which forever changed the face of Palestinian politics.

The Nineteenth PNC adopted two documents—the Political Program and the Declaration of Independence—which, together with Arafat's statements in Geneva a month later, finalize the evolution of the

PLO's peace strategy. In terms of ends and means these three documents are clear and concise. They contain important departures from the preceding programs and, although they all convey the same message, they do so using different idioms. Thus, while the Nineteenth PNC program outlines the objectives of the Palestinian people and the means for achieving them, the Declaration is a solemn and hopeful affirmation of Palestinian principles and aspirations couched in the formal style befitting such an occasion. The significance of Arafat's statement, meanwhile, is that by clarifying the points considered to remain ambiguous by Washington, it led to the initiation of a "substantive dialogue" between the PLO and the United States government.

Together, then, the Political Program of the Nineteenth PNC, the Declaration of an Independent Palestinian State, and Arafat's statement, comprise a single political platform. The ideas put forth in them, marking a departure from the old tactic of ambiguity, are the culmination of the Palestinian peace strategy, embodying with unprecedented clarity the consistency and continuity of PLO grand strategy since it started to move toward peaceful accommodation with an Israel within pre-1967 borders.

The main ideas of the three texts can be summarized as follows:

1. UN Security Council Resolutions 242 and 338 are accepted as the "basis" for convening an international peace conference on the Middle East and the Palestine question. This is the most novel point in the PNC program. Arafat's statement further spells out that the PLO accepts "Resolutions 242 and 338 as the basis for

negotiations *with Israel* within the framework of the international conference" (emphasis added).

2. The General Assembly partition resolution 181 (II) of 1947, the rejection of which was at the very core of the Palestine National Charters, is not merely endorsed in the Declaration of Independence, but cited as a *source of legitimacy* of the Palestine State.

3. Israel is unambiguously recognized not only as a de facto entity but as a legitimate state in the PNC's clear endorsement of the UN General Assembly resolution 181, which partitions Palestine into an Arab and a Jewish state: by grounding the legitimacy of the Palestinian state in this resolution, the PLO by the same token recognizes the legitimacy of the Jewish state. Arafat's statement goes a step further in clarifying previously adopted positions. It talks about the "right of all parties concerned in the Middle East conflict to exist in peace and security, and, as I have mentioned, including the state of Palestine, *Israel* and other neighbors, according to the Resolution [sic] 242 and 338" (emphasis added).

4. A State of Palestine, with its capital at East Jerusalem, is declared on the basis of the United Nations resolution. Although the boundaries of the state are not explicitly spelled out, it is evident that the Palestinian state will be confined to the West Bank and Gaza from section 2, clause (b) of the PNC Political Program, which calls for "Israel's withdrawal from all the Palestinian and Arab territories which it has occupied *since 1967*, including Arab Jerusalem" (emphasis added). This suggests that the PLO has adopted the *principle* of partition rather than the territorial details of UN Resolution 181 of 1947. In other words, the borders of the Palestinian state will include only the West Bank (including East Jerusalem) and Gaza, i.e.,

about 23 percent of Mandatory Palestine. As is evident in the overall thrust of the three texts, partition along these geographic lines will be a final settlement.

5. Diplomacy and peaceful settlement with Israel itself are unambiguously chosen as the means to achieve Palestinian goals. The references to resolutions 181, 242, 338, and other UN resolutions, together with the emphasis on an international peace conference and the total absence of any reference to armed struggle are clear indications of the displacement of diplomacy over military means.

6. Terrorism in all its forms—individual, group, and state—is emphatically rejected. This rejection, affirmed earlier in the Cairo Declaration of 7 November 1985, is explicitly stated in the political program; Arafat in his Geneva statement "renounces" it. However, the PNC Political Program affirms the "right of peoples to resist foreign occupation, colonialism, and racial discrimination, and their right to struggle for their independence," while Arafat's statement stresses that "neither Arafat, nor any[one else] for that matter, can stop the intifada, the uprising," which will come to an end only when the national aims of the Palestinians are realized. Like all national liberation movements throughout history, the PLO was unwilling to give up the right to resistance to occupation.

Thus, the resolutions of the PNC demonstrate a fundamental change in the grand strategy of the PLO, reflecting a sea change in Palestinian politics in general. The consistent evolution of the Palestinian peace strategy, as manifested in the PNC resolutions, indicates that the change is neither transient nor tactical, but a soberly conceived attempt at achieving a peaceful and final settlement with an Israel in its pre-1967 borders. From insisting on regaining all of Palestine to emphasizing an independent state on part of Palestine as a final goal, and from espousing armed struggle exclusively to focusing on diplomacy, the PLO has shown its readiness to negotiate peace.

Because the PNC is the highest policy-making institution of the PLO, and because its resolutions, representing the broadest Palestinian consensus, are accepted as binding guidelines for the PLO Executive Committee, the policies that it recommends are not a fiat decreed by a dominant leader or group but the by-product of an intensive bargaining process involving all Palestinian groups and political opinions. To be sure, no compromise settlement will have unanimous Palestinian support given the pluralist nature of the Palestinian polity. Some Palestinian groups continue to call for unswerving commitment to the National Charter, but these are not at the center of Palestinian power and decision-making. No political community—least of all Israel—is without divisions, socioeconomic disparities, and rejectionists within its ranks.

In the final analysis, what matters is the general trend of thought that shapes the world view of a community. Among the Palestinians, the trend has indisputably been towards pragmatism and coexistence, towards the reshaping of their goals. The Palestinians have made formidable concessions. They have progressively, through twenty-five years of struggle, recognized not merely the existence but the *legitimacy* of a state responsible for the dispossession and eviction of the overwhelming majority of their population. They have renounced forever their claims to over two-thirds of their homeland where, on the eve of Israel's creation, they constituted two-thirds of the population and owned over ninety percent of the land. Through the successive PNCs expressing the views of the great majority of the people, they have expressed their willingness to accept a state on a mere 23 percent of their ancestral soil. They have unambiguously declared themselves ready to come to terms, to live in peace.

The ball is now in Israel's court.

CHRONOLOGY

1947

November 29 —The UN General Assembly, with the backing of the US and USSR, recommends that Palestine be partitioned into a Jewish state, a Palestinian state, and an international enclave which would include Jerusalem

1948

May 15 —British Mandate over Palestine ends

—Declaration of the State of Israel

—First Arab-Israeli war starts

1949

February–
July —Armistice agreements signed

	between Israel and the neighboring Arab states
1949–1964:	—Palestinians in the diaspora lay the foundations for the rebuilding of their shattered community in the form of workers', students', teachers' and women's organizations
	—Fateh, which later formed the centrist backbone of the PLO, works underground to reconstruct the bases of Palestinian identity
	—Tens of Palestinian groups spring up to stress self-reliance and champion the goals of return and total liberation
1952	
July 23	—A revolutionary government comes to power in Egypt
1956	
October 29	—Israel, England and France attack Egypt
1958	
February 1	—Syria and Egypt form the United Arab Republic
July 14	—The Iraqi monarchy is overthrown

July 15	—U.S. Marines are sent to Lebanon

1961
September 30	—The union between Syria and Egypt is dissolved

1962
September 29	—A revolution takes place in Yemen

1964
January	—First Arab Summit Conference creates the PLO, under its own auspices
May 28–June 2	—First Palestine National Council meets in Jerusalem and drafts the Palestinian National Charter

1965
May 31–June 4	—The Second PNC meets in Cairo
1965–1966	—Non-PLO Palestinian groups, notably Fateh, carry out guerrilla activities against Israel

1966
May 20–24	—The Third PNC meets in Gaza

1967
June 5	—The Six-Day War of 1967 breaks out

	—Israel occupies East Jerusalem, the West Bank and the Gaza Strip, as well as Sinai and the Golan Heights
	—About 300,000 Palestinians become refugees, many for the second time
November 22	—The UN Security Council passes Resolution 242

1968

March	—The PLO agrees to give the commando groups half of the seats in a new PNC
March 21	—The Israeli army incurs many casualties in an attack on a Fateh base in the Jordan valley at Karameh, within Jordanian territory
July 10–17	—The Fourth PNC meets in Cairo
October 10	—Salah Khalaf (Abu Iyad), the second highest official in Fateh after Yasir Arafat, expresses his support for the concept of a secular democratic state in Palestine

1969

February 1–4	—The Fifth PNC meets in Cairo. Fateh leader Yasir Arafat

	is elected as Chairman of the Executive Committee
September 1–6	—The Sixth PNC meets in Cairo

1970

February	—Clashes between the Palestinian commando groups and the Jordanian army
May 30–June 4	—The Seventh PNC meets in Cairo
June	—The crisis between the commando groups and the Jordanian army escalates
July	—Egyptian president Gamal Abd al-Nasir and King Hussein of Jordan accept U.S. Secretary of State Rogers' peace plan, calling for the implementation of UN Security Council Resolution 242
August 28	—Emergency Session of the PNC in Amman
September	—Radical Palestinian groups enter into a confrontation with the Jordanian government. The Popular Front for the Liberation of Palestine (PFLP) hijacks civilian airplanes and takes them to an airport in Jordan. Confrontation between the PLO and the Jordanian army

1971

February 28-March 5	—The Eighth PNC meets in Cairo
July	—Renewed confrontation between the PLO and Jordan ends in the expulsion of the PLO from Jordan
July 7–13	—The Ninth PNC meets in Cairo
November 28	—Black September, a Fateh offshoot, assassinates Wasfi al-Tall, the Jordanian Prime Minister, in Cairo

1972

March 15	—King Hussein declares his United Kingdom Plan, which envisages a Jordanian/Palestinian federation. Most Arab countries attack this plan
April 6–12	—The Tenth PNC meets in Cairo, condemns King Hussein's plan and calls for his overthrow. Egypt severs diplomatic relations with Jordan
July	—Egyptian President Anwar al-Sadat expells Soviet military advisors from Egypt
September 5–6	—Black September kidnaps members of the Israeli Olympic

team in Munich, many of whom die in a shootout with Israeli security agents

1973

January 6–12	—The Eleventh PNC meets in Cairo
April 10	—An Israeli military squad assassinates three top PLO officials in Beirut
October	—Egypt and Syria attack Israel; an oil embargo is imposed by the oil-producing Arab states

1974

January 18	—The first disengagement agreement between Egypt and Israel is signed
May 31	—A disengagement agreement between Syria and Israel is signed that establishes an armistice line in the Golan Heights
June 1–9	—The Twelfth PNC meets in Cairo
October 26–28	—At the Rabat Summit Conference Arab heads of state recognize the PLO as the sole legitimate representative of the Palestinian people
November 13	—Yasir Arafat addresses the UN General Assembly

November 22	—The PLO is given observer status at the United Nations

1975

April 13	—Maronite militiamen ambush a bus passing through 'Ayn al-Rummaneh, a Christian suburb of Beirut, massacring the twenty-eight passengers (most of whom are Palestinians) on board. The Lebanese civil war begins
September 4	—The second Israeli-Egyptian disengagement agreement is signed
September	—U.S. Secretary of State Kissinger commits the United States not to recognize or negotiate with the PLO unless it accepts UN Security Council Resolution 242 and recognizes Israel's right to exist

1976

April	—Pro-PLO Palestinian nationalists win the municipal elections in the West Bank
June 1	—Syrian troops enter Lebanon and take sides with the Maronite militias against the Lebanese left and its Palestinian allies
July 21	—Dr. Isam Sartawi, a PLO

official, meets in Paris with retired Israeli general Matityahu Peled, this being one of the first secret meetings between PLO officials and Israelis interested in a compromise settlement with the Palestinians

1977

March 12–20	—The Thirteenth PNC meets in Cairo
May 17	—Menachem Begin elected Prime Minister of Israel
October 1	—The United States and Soviet Union propose to convene a Geneva Conference in order to resolve the Palestinian question and insure "the legimimate rights of the Palestinian people"
November 19	—Sadat visits Jerusalem

1978

March 15	—Israel invades Lebanon
September 17	—The Camp David accords are signed
November 5	—The Arab Summit in Baghdad condemns Camp David and calls for a Palestinian state and a comprehensive Arab-Israeli settlement that would keep Israel contained within its pre-1967 borders

1979

January 15–23	—The Fourteenth PNC meets in Damascus
February	—The Shah of Iran is overthrown and the Islamic Revolution led by Ayatollah Khomeini is victorious
March 26	—Signing of the Egyptian-Israeli peace treaty
July 6–8	—Yasir Arafat meets with Austrian Chancellor Bruno Kreisky and Willy Brandt of West Germany
September 19	—Arafat meets with King Hussein in Amman and reportedly discusses the idea of a Jordanian-Palestinian confederation

1980

June 13	—The European Economic Community (EEC), meeting in Venice, adopts the Venice Declaration, which recognizes the Palestinians' right to self-determination, calls for a multilateral framework for peace negotiations, and criticizes Israel's occupation and its settlement policies
July 30	—Israel annexes East Jerusalem

September	—War breaks out between Iran and Iraq

1981

February 23	—Leonid Brezhnev outlines a Soviet peace proposal which calls for comprehensive peace, a Palestinian state, and security guarantees for all states in the region, including Israel
April 11–19	—The Fifteenth PNC meets in Damascus
June 6	—Israeli jet fighters bomb an Iraqi nuclear reactor in Baghdad
July	—Israel escalates its military attacks on the Lebanese border and carries out massive air raids against Palestinian refugee camps in Beirut
August 7	—Crown Prince Fahd (later King Fahd) of Saudi Arabia proposes an eight-point peace plan which calls for the establishment of a Palestinian state in the West Bank and Gaza and implicitly recognizes Israel within its pre-1947 borders. The PLO welcomes the Fahd plan
October 6	—An Egyptian Islamic group assassinates Anwar al-Sadat and

	Husni Mubarak becomes president of Egypt
December 14	—Israel formally annexes the Golan Heights

1982

June 6	—Israel invades Lebanon with the purpose of dismantling the PLO and destroying the infrastructure of the Palestinians in Lebanon
August 21	—The PLO leaves Beirut under the protection of a multinational force
September 1	—United States President Reagan outlines a peace proposal for the Middle East which calls for a self-governing Palestinian entity in the West Bank and Gaza in some kind of association with Jordan. Israel rejects the plan; the PLO adopts a reserved position
September 8	—The Arab Summit in Fez adopts a peace plan whose basic contours were outlined in the Fahd plan of August 1981
September 16–18	—Hundreds of Palestinians are massacred in the Beirut refugee camps of Sabra and Shatila by Maronite militiamen with the connivance of the Israeli army

1983

February 22	—The Sixteenth PNC meets in Algiers
May	—Fateh dissidents in Lebanon rebel against Arafat with Syrian backing
October 10	—Yitzhak Shamir takes office as Israeli Prime Minister
December 20	—Arafat and his supporters are forced to leave Tripoli, Lebanon, after being encircled by Fateh dissidents supported by Syrian troops
December 22	—Arafat meets Egyptian President Husni Mubarak, paving the way for closer Egyptian-PLO ties. Dissidents from the PFLP, DFLP and Fateh strongly condemn the meeting

1984

September 14	—Shimon Peres takes office as Israeli Prime Minister
November 22–28	—The Seventeenth PNC meets in Amman, calling for an independent Palestinian state in confederation with Jordan

1985

February 11	—King Hussein and Arafat announce the Amman Agreement, which calls for the forma-

	tion of a joint Jordanian-Palestinian delegation in peace talks on the basis of UN Security Council Resolution 242 and the establishment of an independent Palestinian state in confederation with Jordan
November 7	—Arafat declares in Cairo his renunciation of terrorism

1986

February 19	—King Hussein abrogates the Amman Agreement
October 20	—Yitzhak Shamir takes office as Israeli Prime Minister

1987

March 16	—Major Palestinian commando groups sign the Tunis Document, which stipulates points of agreement among them. These points are: the establishment of an independent Palestinian state, commitment to the Fez peace plan, and the rejection of the Amman Agreement
April 20–25	—The PNC holds its Eighteenth meeting in Algiers
December 9	—The Palestinian Uprising (Intifada) begins on a mass scale in the West Bank and Gaza

1988

April 16	—Israeli agents assassinate PLO military leader Khalil al-Wazir (Abu Jihad) at his home in Tunis
June 7	—Bassam Abu Sharif, special advisor to Arafat, distributes a position paper at the Arab summit meeting in Algiers on the prospects of a Palestinian-Israeli settlement
June 30	—Prominent American Jews consider the Abu Sharif paper to be a very positive contribution to the cause of peace
August 20	—Cease-fire between Iraq and Iran goes into effect
November 12–15	—The Nineteenth PNC meets in Algiers and issues the Palestinian Declaration of Independence
November 26	—The U.S. State Department refuses to issue a visa to Arafat so that he may address the UN in New York
December 13	—The UN General Assembly convenes in Geneva to hear Arafat's address
December 14	—Arafat accepts UN Security Council Resolution 242, accepts the right of Israel to exist, and

renounces terrorism. The United States government authorizes the opening of a "substantive dialogue" with the PLO

NOTES

1. The findings of the poll, which was co-sponsored by the East Jerusalem daily *al-Fajr*, the American newspaper *Newsday*, and the Australian Broadcasting Corporation, were published in *The Jerusalem Post International Edition*, September 13–20, 1986.
2. *New York Times*, March 21, 1989; see also *The Jerusalem Post International Edition*, no. 1,440, June 11, 1988.
3. For relevant details see Laurie A. Brand, *Palestinians in the Arab World: Institution Building and the Search for State* (New York: Columbia University Press, 1988), pp. 1–40; Cheryl Rubenberg, *The Palestine Liberation Organization: Its Institutional Infrastructure* (Belmont, Mass.: Institute of Arab Studies, 1983); Asad Abdul-Rahman and Rashid Hamid, "The Palestine Liberation Organization: Past, Present, and Future" (paper presented at the First United Nations Seminar on the Question of Palestine, July 14–18, 1980; United Nations Publication 168); Rashid Hamid, "What is the PLO?" *Journal of Palestine Studies*, vol. IV, no. 4, Summer 1975, pp. 90–109.
4. For works on this subject based on recently declassified Israeli archival material, see: Benny Morris, *The Birth of the Palestinian Refugee Problem, 1947–1949* (Cambridge: Cambridge University Press, 1987); Simha Flapan, *The Birth of Israel: Myths and Realities* (New York: Pantheon Books, 1987); Tom Segev, *1949: The First Israelis* (New York: Free Press, 1986); Avi Shlaim, *Collusion Across the Jordan: King Abdullah, the Zionist Movement, and the Partition of Palestine* (Oxford: Oxford University Press, 1988). See also the special issue of the *Journal of Palestine Studies* on the same subject, vol. XVIII, no. 69, Autumn 1988.

5. For background information see Helena Cobban, *The Palestinian Liberation Organization: People, Power and Politics* (Cambridge: Cambridge University Press, 1984); William B. Quandt, Fuad Jabber, and Ann Mosely Lesch, *The Politics of Palestinian Nationalism* (Berkeley: University of California Press, 1973); Isa al-Shu'aybi, *Al-Kiyaniyyah al-Filastiniyyah: al-Wa'i al-Dhati wa al-Tatawwur al-Mu'assasati* [Palestinian Statism: Entity Consciousness and Institutional Development] (Beirut: PLO Research Center, 1979).
6. For an elaboration of this point, see Malcolm H. Kerr, *The Arab Cold War: Gamal Abd al-Nasir and His Rivals, 1958–1970* (Oxford: Oxford University Press, 1971), pp. 114–17.
7. See Brand, *Palestinians in the Arab World*, Chapter Four.
8. Ahmad Baha' al-Din, *Iqtirah Dawlat Filastin* [*The Suggestion of a State of Palestine*] (Beirut: Dar al-Tali'ah, 1968).
9. For details on this organization, see Emile Sahliyeh, *In Search of Leadership: West Bank Politics Since 1967* (Washington, D.C.: The Brookings Institution, 1988), pp. 42–69.
10. See Helena Cobban, "Palestinian Peace Plans," in Willard A. Beling (ed.), *Middle East Peace Plans* (New York: St. Martin's Press, 1986), pp. 43–44.
11. See Galia Golan, *The Soviet Union and the Palestine Liberation Organization* (New York: Praeger, 1980), pp. 50–112; Galia Golan, "Gorbachev's Middle East Strategy" *Foreign Affairs*, vol. 66, no. 1, Fall 1987, pp. 45–46.
12. For details on PLO-Jordanian relations, see Sahliyeh, *In Search of Leadership*, pp. 98–112, 170–75 and Arthur R. Day, *East Bank/West Bank: Jordan and the Prospects for Peace* (New York: Council on Foreign Relations, 1986), pp. 112–41.
13. In this period, particularly from December 1976 to May 1977, numerous meetings took place between members of the central core of Fateh and avowed Zionist personalities, including a number of Israelis. In late 1974, arrangements were made for a meeting between Arafat and Nahum Goldman, the president of the World Zionist Organization at the time. Because of the strong pressure of the Israeli government the meeting never took place. For an account of these contacts, which produced nothing, mainly as a result of the Israeli government's intransigence and the debilitating effect of the Lebanese civil war on the PLO, see Alain Gresh, *The PLO: The Struggle Within* (London: Zed Books Ltd., 1985), pp. 195–99, and the monthly Paris journal *Israel et Palestine*

for the months extending from December 1977 to February 1978, as well as the French daily *Le Monde* of 6 and 11 January 1977. More detailed accounts can be found in Seth Tillman, *The United States in the Middle East* (Bloomington: Indiana University Press, 1982), p. 213 ff.; Noam Chomsky's articles in *New Politics* (Winter 1975–76, Winter 1978–79), and his book *Towards a New Cold War* (New York: Pantheon, 1982), Chapters 9 and 13.